Our Emotions and Behaviour

Not Fair, Won't Share

Written by Sue Graves

Illustrated by Desideria Guicciardini

W

FRANKLIN WATTS

LONDON · SYDNEY

On Monday, Miss Clover had a surprise for everyone. She had made a Space Station.

There were **buttons** to **push**.
There were **levers** to **pull**.
There were boots and a helmet
to wear, too!

Only three children could play at a time.
But **everyone** wanted a turn!

Then Miss Clover had a good idea.
She put everyone's name in a hat.

She pulled out Posy's name first.

She pulled out Ben's name second.

She pulled out Alfie's name third.

Miss Clover said they could play first.
But they had to **take turns** and to **share**.

Posy put on the boots and the helmet.

She pushed all the
buttons.

She pulled all the
levers.

She wouldn't let Ben or Alfie take turns.

She wouldn't let them wear the **boots** or the **helmet.**

Ben got **cross.**
He said it wasn't fair.
He pushed **Posy hard!**

Alfie got **cross.**
He said it wasn't fair.
He snatched **the helmet!**

Posy got very, **very cross!**
She said it wasn't fair.
She said she **didn't** want to share!

Miss Clover got **cross.**
She sent them out.

Posy went to the Reading Corner.
Soon she stopped feeling cross.
She wished that she had taken turns
to play with Alfie and Ben.

Ben went to the Art Corner.
Soon he stopped feeling cross.
He wished that he had not
pushed Posy.

Alfie went on the computer. Soon he stopped feeling cross. He wished that he had not snatched the helmet.

Miss Clover counted slowly to ten.
Soon she stopped feeling cross, too!

Posy, Ben and Alfie said sorry
to Miss Clover and to each other.

Miss Clover let them have another turn
in the Space Station.

She told them to **take turns** and to **share**.

They all took turns to push the **buttons.**

They all took turns to pull the **levers.**

They all shared the **helmet** and the **boots.**

They had lots of **fun.**

And this time, no one got cross at **all!**

Can you tell the story of what happens when these two aliens find a toy they don't want to share?

How do you think they felt when they didn't share the toy? How did they feel at the end?

A note about sharing this book

The *Our Emotions and Behaviour* series has been developed to provide a starting point for further discussion on children's feelings and behaviour, both in relation to themselves and to other people.

Not Fair, Won't Share
This story explores sharing in a reassuring way. It examines the problems that can arise when people don't share – especially the angry response that being selfish can generate. It also looks how people can stop feeling angry.

The book aims to encourage children to work as a group or class, taking turns and sharing fairly. It promotes awareness of behavioural expectations in a setting and of the consequences of their words and actions for themselves and others. The book also explores how to express and control feelings in appropriate ways.

Storyboard puzzle
The wordless storyboard on pages 26 and 27 provides an opportunity for speaking and listening. Children are encouraged to tell the story illustrated in the panels: when two little aliens find a toy, they each want it. One snatches it away, then the other snatches it back. But it is not until the aliens share the toy that playing with it becomes fun.

How to use the book
The book is designed for adults to share with either an individual child, or a group of children, and as a starting point for discussion.

The book also provides visual support and repeated words and phrases to build confidence in children who are starting to read on their own.

Before reading the story
Choose a time to read when you and the children are relaxed and have time to share the story.

Spend time looking at the illustrations and talk about what the book may be about before reading it together.

After reading, talk about the book with the children.

- What was it about? Have the children ever been selfish when playing with others? Why do they think it is important to share and to let others take turns?

- Extend this discussion by talking about other things that children find hard to share. Do they find it hard to share toys with friends or with siblings? What things do they like / dislike about sharing with others? Remind them it may not only be material things that they find hard to share. They may, for example, find it hard to share a parent's attention with a sibling.

- Talk about the steps each character took to stop feeling angry. Point out that adults too feel angry and have to find ways of controlling their feelings.

- Talk about the things that make them feel angry. Spend time discussing ways of controlling anger. Some may find it best to leave the room, count to ten or distract themselves with another activity. Encourage the children to share their experiences and their tried and tested solutions for anger management.

- Talk about the importance of saying "sorry" to the person who is upset by their actions, and how this can make the person feel better.

- Look at the storyboard puzzle. Talk about how each little alien felt when the other would not share the toy.

  Talk about other things that are better to share than to have or play with on their own.

  Play a game that involves sharing and taking turns, such as a simple card or board game. Or sing a round such as *London's Burning* or *Frère Jacques*.

This edition 2014

Franklin Watts
338 Euston Road
London
NW1 3BH

Franklin Watts Australia
Level 17/207 Kent Street
Sydney
NSW 2000

A CIP catalogue record for this book is available
from the British Library.

ISBN 978 1 4451 2991 4 (paperback)
ISBN 978 1 4451 2129 1 (library ebook)

Editors: Adrian Cole and Jackie Hamley
Designer: Peter Scoulding and Jonathan Hair

Printed in China

Franklin Watts is a division of
Hachette Children's Books,
an Hachette UK company.
www.hachette.co.uk